About Skill Builders
Reading
Comprehension Grade 3

Welcome to Skill Builders *Reading Comprehension* for third grade. This book is designed to improve children's reading comprehension skills through focused practice. The book's eye-catching graphics and engaging topics entice even reluctant readers. Each full-color workbook contains grade-level-appropriate passages and exercises based on national standards to help ensure that children master basic skills before progressing.

More than 70 pages of activities cover essential comprehension strategies, such as inferring, sequencing, and finding the main idea and supporting details. The workbook also contains questions and activities to help children build their vocabularies.

The Skill Builders series offers workbooks that are perfect for keeping skills sharp during the school year or preparing them for the next grade.

Credits:

Content Editors: Ashley Anderson and Elizabeth Swenson
Copy Editor: Sandra Shoffner
Layout, Cover Design, and Inside Illustrations: Nick Greenwood

carsondellosa.com
Carson-Dellosa Publishing, LLC
Greensboro, North Carolina

Printed in the USA • All rights reserved.

ISBN 978-1-936023-31-8
09-214161151

Table of Contents

Suggested Reading List

Adler, David A.
Cam Jansen: The Mystery of the Television Dog

Blume, Judy
Friend or Fiend with the Pain and the Great One

Burns, Marilyn
Spaghetti and Meatballs for All!

Burton, Virginia Lee
Katy and the Big Snow

Carle, Eric
The Tiny Seed

Catling, Patrick Skene
The Chocolate Touch

Cleary, Beverly
Ramona Quimby, Age 8

Cole, Joanna
The Magic School Bus Lost in the Solar System

Dahl, Roald
Fantastic Mr. Fox

Danziger, Paula
Amber Brown Is Not a Crayon

dePaola, Tomie
The Art Lesson

DK Publishing
Eye Wonder: Mammals
Eye Wonder: Invention

Estes, Eleanor
The Hundred Dresses

George, Jean Craighead
The Tarantula in My Purse and 172 Other Wild Pets

Goldish, Meish
Does the Moon Change Shape?

Gregory, Kristiana
Across the Wide and Lonesome Prairie: The Oregon Trail Diary of Hattie Campbell, 1847

Hidaka, Masako
Girl from the Snow Country

Keats, Ezra Jack
Peter's Chair

Jeschke, Susan
Perfect the Pig

Jukes, Mavis
Blackberries in the Dark

Kellogg, Steven
Paul Bunyan
Chicken Little

Lansky, Bruce (ed.)
The Best of Girls to the Rescue: Tales of Clever, Courageous Girls from Around the World

Lerner, Carol
Butterflies in the Garden

Locker, Thomas
Cloud Dance

MacDonald, Betty
Mrs. Piggle-Wiggle

McMullan, Kate
Dinosaur Hunters

Pratt, Kristin Joy
A Walk in the Rainforest

Schroeder, Alan
Minty: A Story of Young Harriet Tubman

Seuss, Dr.
The Lorax

Silverstein, Shel
A Light in the Attic

Smith, Robert Kimmel
Chocolate Fever

St. George, Judith
So You Want to Be President?

Steig, William
The Amazing Bone
Sylvester and the Magic Pebble

Waters, Kate
Samuel Eaton's Day: A Day in the Life of a Pilgrim Boy
Sarah Morton's Day: A Day in the Life of a Pilgrim Girl

White, E. B.
Charlotte's Web

Stay Safe

Read the passage. Then, write _T_ if a statement is true. Write _F_ if a statement is false.

Trains go almost everywhere. There are more than 200,000 miles (321,868 km) of track in the United States. Maybe there is even a train track near your home. You need to learn a few rules that will keep you safe.

When you need to cross a train track, be sure to go to a specially marked crossing. Pay attention to all of the signs. Never go around a gate that is down. Never cross the tracks when lights are flashing. Trains can be very fast and very quiet. You may not hear one coming until it is close. Plus, trains run at all times, even at night.

Trains are big and heavy. If something is on the tracks when a train is coming, the engineer has a hard time seeing it. Even if an engineer sees the object, it can take the engineer more than 1 mile (1.61 km) to stop a train!

Remember: Cross only at special crossings. Watch all of the signs. Do not ever play near train tracks. Stay safe!

1. _____ One purpose of "Stay Safe" is to teach you how to ride a bike.

2. _____ One purpose of "Stay Safe" is to give the history of trains.

3. _____ One purpose of "Stay Safe" is to teach safety rules for train tracks.

4. _____ One purpose of "Stay Safe" is to keep you from getting hurt by trains.

5. _____ One purpose of "Stay Safe" is to sell train tickets.

6. _____ One purpose of "Stay Safe" is to tell the exact times that trains run.

7. _____ One purpose of "Stay Safe" is to make you pay attention around train tracks.

Costume Day

Read the story. Then, answer the questions.

Rosa had wanted just one thing ever since her first year at Washington Street School. She wanted to win the Costume Day contest.

Costume Day was on a Saturday in April. Everyone came. There were game booths, balloons, and many good things to eat.

The best part of the day was the costume contest. A winner was chosen for every grade. There was also a grand prize. This year the prize was a free pass to the zoo.

Rosa thought about her costume all year. She looked at books and magazines to get ideas. She looked in shops and catalogs too. Most of the kids wanted premade costumes. Rosa wanted hers to be special. She wanted a costume that was different from all of her friends' costumes.

One day, Rosa was doing a report on mammals for her science class. She saw a picture that gave her an idea for her perfect costume. She bought a striped tail and ears with her birthday money. Then, she painted a white stripe on a black leotard. Next, she painted paws on an old pair of black shoes. Last, Rosa collected bottles of perfume from some of her neighbors and from her grandmother.

At last, the great day came.

1. What animal costume did Rosa wear?

   _____

2. Circle **cause** or **effect** below each sentence.

   A **cause** is something that creates a result. That result is called the **effect**.

   When Rosa got to the school playground, all of the other children screamed and ran away.

           cause   **effect**

   Rosa put on her costume and used all of the perfume.

           cause   **effect**

3. What does Rosa want?

   _____

   _____

4. Do you think Rosa will win the costume contest? Why or why not?

   _____

   _____

Alexa Jones, Private Eye

Read the story. Then, answer the questions.

Alexa hung a sign outside her clubhouse door. It read:

Alexa Jones, Private Eye

Her neighbor, Noah, rode carefully down the driveway on his bike. He was still wobbly without his training wheels. He looked at her sign for a long time. Then, he looked around the yard. "Where is the yard sale?" he asked.

"There is no yard sale," Alexa told him. "The sign says that I am a detective. I solve crimes, like finding things that are lost."

"If I lost something, could you find it?" Noah asked.

"I could try," said Alexa.

Alexa and Noah went to his house. They went into his room, and Alexa looked around. She was not surprised that Noah had lost something. In fact, she was surprised that he ever found anything. Noah opened his closet. He took out a plastic car with a slot in it.

"This is my bank," he said. "Every week, I get 10 dimes for my allowance. I spend five of them at the mall. Then, I put the other five in here. On Monday, I had a lot of dimes. Now, they are all gone. Can you find them for me?"

"We need some clues," Alexa said, shaking the bank. She did not hear any dimes. She opened the door on the bottom of the bank. Two pieces of paper fell out. One was white, and one was green. Something was written on the white paper. Alexa read it and tried not to laugh. The note read:

Dear Noah: I needed change to do the laundry. You had $4.50 in dimes. Here is $5.00. Love, Mom.

1. About how old is Noah?
   A. five years old
   B. two years old
   C. eight years old

2. What clues do you have about Noah's age?

   _____

   _____

3. Noah thought the sign said " _____ ."

4. Was Noah's room messy or neat? How do you know?

   _____

   _____

   _____

5. The green piece of paper in Noah's bank was a _____

   _____ .

6. Does Noah's mom have a washing machine at their house?

   _____

   How do you know?

   _____

   _____

Roberto's Robot

Read the paragraph. Then, number the events in the order that they happened.

No one has seen Roberto for hours. He has been in the basement building a robot. Roberto's family is going to be surprised when they see the robot. Roberto hopes they will not be mad. Roberto used the trash can for the robot's body. He used a shoe box for the head. One of his Mom's flowerpots made the perfect hat. He added a flyswatter to make one arm and a broom to make the other. Roberto used some large nuts and bolts to make the robot's eyes and nose. Then, he painted a smile on the robot with his sister's nail polish. Roberto thinks his robot is terrific! He hopes his family will think so too.

_____ Roberto used a flowerpot for the hat.

_____ Roberto used nail polish to draw a smile.

_____ Roberto used a trash can for the body.

_____ Roberto used nuts and bolts to make the robot's eyes and nose.

_____ Roberto made one arm from a flyswatter.

_____ Roberto used a shoe box to make the robot's head.

Be a Context Detective

Use the context clues in each sentence to find the meaning of each bold word. Circle your answers.

Context clues are words or phrases that help you learn the meaning of other words.

1. It was a **pleasant** day. The sky was blue and the sun was warm. We put on our swimsuits and ran down to the beach.

   A. dull   B. nice   C. sad

2. It was a nice, spring day. Mario went to gather some eggs. The hens were **mining** for bugs and worms in the yard.

   A. playing   B. digging   C. jumping

3. Malia fell in the yard at lunch. She hurt her arm. The **injury** got worse when she carried a heavy box for Ms. Garcia.

   A. dream   B. page   C. wound

4. Some dinosaurs were small, but brachiosaurs were **enormous**. They were taller than some trees!

   A. fast   B. big   C. old

5. We would not let a little rain **spoil** our trip to the zoo. We took our raincoats and umbrellas.

   A. ruin   B. fix   C. share

Seeds, Seeds, Seeds!

Read the passage. Then, answer the questions.

Many plants begin their lives as seeds. Flowers, garden vegetables, and trees all have seeds. If you have ever soaked a lima bean in water and then cut it in half, you have seen a baby plant inside of a seed.

Seeds come in many sizes. A coconut is a very big seed. Coconuts float on the ocean to new islands where they can grow into palm trees. Palm trees are big, but big plants do not always come from big seeds. A redwood, one of the biggest trees in the world, grows from a very tiny seed.

After seeds leave the plant, they need a good place to grow. A willow seed needs to land quickly in a good place. After a few days, the baby willow tree inside the seed dies. Most seeds last much longer than willow seeds. The seeds of one date palm grew after 2,000 years!

1. What does a coconut grow into? _____

2. Do all big plants come from big seeds? _____

3. What carries a coconut to a new island? _____

4. Name one of the biggest trees in the world? _____

5. How long did one date palm seed stay alive? _____

What Is the Main Idea?

Read each paragraph. Then, circle the main idea.

1. Toucans are social birds. In the rain forest, they live in flocks of six or more birds. They look for homes in hollow trees. Then, they all sleep together in one big nest inside the tree. When toucans have babies, both the mother and the father sit on the eggs and feed the chicks. The toucan's friendly nature makes it easy to tame when it lives in a zoo.

   A. Toucans are friendly animals.
   B. Toucans love their babies.
   C. Toucans do not like the rain forest.

2. Giraffes are gentle animals that always travel in herds. When you see a giraffe on an African plain, it looks like it is alone. It is not. Giraffes can see over half of a mile away because they are so tall. As long as they can see the other animals in their family, they feel safe. Giraffes will moo, hiss, and whistle to "talk" to each other as they eat.

   A. Giraffes are afraid to walk on the plains.
   B. Giraffes like to travel alone.
   C. Giraffes always travel in groups.

Title, Please

Read each newspaper article. Choose the best title for each article from the word bank.

Prowler Caught by Police

Dinosaur Wins Dream House!

Big Mystery Solved!

Time Runs Out for Della's Drive

Local Author Writes Book!

Write the title on the line above the article.

_____

1. The place was Mudrock. It was 12:02 A.M. last Saturday night. Rangers in Sandstone Park found huge, mysterious footprints. Scientists looked at the prints. No one knew who made the prints. They were not like the prints of any dinosaur in town. The excitement grew with each day. Yesterday, Dino Dinosaur made an announcement. He made the prints with a bucket and a broom handle!

_____

2. Danny Dinosaur got a big surprise this week. Six weeks ago, Danny entered the Dinosaur Dream House Drawing. The drawing took place last Monday in Flatrock. Danny and his family were surprised and pleased to find they had won. "We just cannot believe it!" Danny told reporters.

3. Debbie Dinosaur has written a book about dinosaur dancing. Her friends in Pebblebrook are very proud. The book is called *Dinosaur Dancing for Beginners*. The book is selling well. Ms. Dinosaur is working on her second book. It will be called *Cooking in a Cave*.

4. The dinosaurs in Dino Town know Della Dinosaur. She is collecting money. Della has been collecting money for the last three months. She will use the money to help dinosaurs in need. Tuesday is the last day for the fund drive. Please help Della get more money! If you want to help, please call Della at 555-2121.

5. The dinosaurs in Slateville will sleep easier tonight. The prowler has been caught. Police were stumped. For six weeks, residents had seen the shadow of the prowler near their windows and doors at night. Nothing was harmed, but the dinosaurs were nervous. The prowler turned out to be little Andy Apatosaurus. Police learned that Andy was walking in his sleep. Andy could not be reached for comment.

A Class Trip to the Zoo

Read the story. Then, answer the questions.

Dylan's class took a trip to the zoo. The zoo was divided into sections. Each section was a different kind of habitat. A **habitat** is a place where animals live. Different animals live in each habitat. Different plants grow in each habitat too.

The class visited animals from the mountains first. This section was called the Mountain Habitat. Dylan's class saw bears, deer, elk, and mountain goats. They learned that not many animals live high in the mountains. Not many plants live high in the mountains either.

The next section the class visited had animals from the forest. This section was called the Forest Habitat. Dylan's class saw wolves, owls, and porcupines. The class learned that some of the animals that live in the mountains also live in the forest.

Next, the class went to the Tropical Forest Habitat. This habitat was like the Forest Habitat, but it was warmer and had more rain. They saw gorillas, parrots, and crocodiles. The gorillas were fun to watch. They ran around and played with their food.

The last section of the zoo had animals from the grasslands. This section was called the Grassland Habitat. Many of the animals that lived in the Grassland Habitat came from Africa. Dylan's class saw giraffes, lions, elephants, and zebras. The class liked the lions the best. They were napping in the shade of a big tree.

1. What does the word **habitat** mean?

   A. an apartment
   B. a place where animals live
   C. being late

2. In which section did Dylan's class see the giraffes?

   A. forest
   B. mountains
   C. grasslands

3. In which section did Dylan's class see the gorillas?

   A. grasslands
   B. tropical forest
   C. mountains

4. In which section did Dylan's class see the porcupines?

   A. mountains
   B. forest
   C. grasslands

Synonyms

Read each sentence. Then, circle the synonym for each bold word.

A **synonym** is a word that means the same thing as another word.

1. Lily did not **recognize** her cousin after he got his hair cut.

   A. forget   B. know   C. think

2. All of the children will **benefit** from having a new playground in the neighborhood.

   A. lose   B. bounce   C. gain

3. The horses waited patiently in the **corral** while the farmers prepared their food.

   A. pen   B. house   C. water

4. Before we go to the zoo, we should **coordinate** our plans with Jason and Eli so that we can meet them there.

   A. practice   B. confuse   C. match

5. Everyone says that the **majestic** scenery of the mountains will take your breath away.

   A. boring   B. grand   C. plain

Antonyms

Read each sentence. Then, circle the antonym for each bold word.

An **antonym** is a word that is the opposite of another word.

1. The **courageous** firefighters rushed to the scene of the fire.
    A. fearful   B. brave   C. positive

2. Whenever we go on a car trip, I always enjoy watching the **scenic** views outside the window.
    A. ugly   B. beautiful   C. simple

3. Henry treats his bicycle like it is **worthless**. He always leaves it outside in the rain.
    A. cheap   B. valuable   C. pretty

4. Carrie was **frantic** as she searched for her homework while the bus was pulling up to her house.
    A. angry   B. panicked   C. calm

5. The spacecraft's **external** fuel tank falls off once it is empty.
    A. inside   B. outside   C. middle

Cockroaches

Read the passage. Then, write _F_ if a statement is a fact. Write _O_ if a statement is an opinion.

> A **fact** is a detail that is real and can be proven. An **opinion** is a belief that is personal and cannot be proven.

Cockroaches have been around for a very long time. They have been on Earth for millions of years. They were here before the dinosaurs. Cockroaches have hard shells. These shells act like armor for cockroaches. Cockroaches also have good hearing and eyesight. Most cockroaches live for about one year. A female cockroach hatches more than 100 baby cockroaches in her short life. Cockroaches eat almost anything. They can live for weeks without food. They can even go days without water. Cockroaches do not bite or sting. So, why do many people scream and run when they see them?

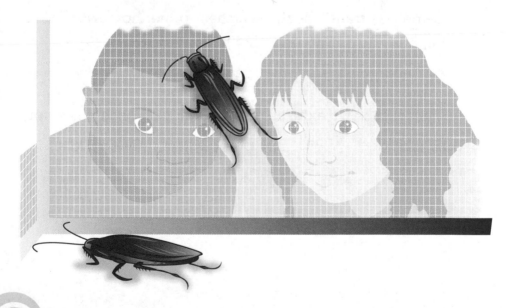

1. _____ Cockroaches have hard shells.

2. _____ Cockroaches have good eyesight.

3. _____ Cockroaches are ugly.

4. _____ Cockroaches eat almost anything.

5. _____ Cockroaches do not bite humans.

Write one detail from the story in each oval to complete the story web. The main idea and one detail have been done for you.

Hard shells act like armor.

Cockroaches have survived on Earth for a long time.

Ellen Ochoa

Read the passage. Then, complete the graphic organizer with details from the passage.

When Ellen Ochoa was growing up, she did not dream of going into space. At that time, there were no female astronauts in America. It was not until Ochoa was 20 years old that Sally Ride and five other women joined the space program. Ochoa was in college then. She applied to become an astronaut. She was picked to join the space program in 1990.

Ochoa was the first Hispanic American woman to fly into space. Her first mission was in 1993. She was in space for nine days. It was Ochoa's job to launch a satellite. She used the shuttle's robot arm to do this. She also helped her team do research. She stayed in touch with her family on Earth using e-mail.

Since that first trip, Ochoa has gone into space three more times. She has spent 978 hours in space. On each trip, she worked the robot arm. Ochoa loves going into space. She thinks it is exciting and interesting.

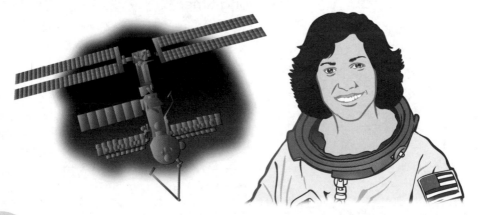

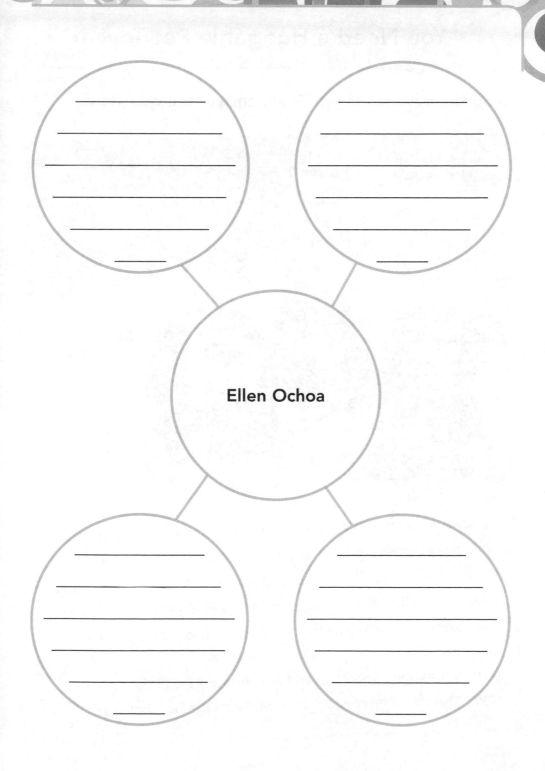

Ellen Ochoa

You Need a Huggable Pet Toy!

Read the advertisement. Then, answer the questions.

Everyone should experience the joy of having a pet! You will love your Huggable Pet toy even more because you never need to feed or bathe it. It snuggles with you. It comes when you call it. Your Huggable Pet even does tricks. Choose your favorite: monkey, dog, cat, or bird. It is worth the joy at any price!

(Prices may vary. Some assembly is required. Clothes, pet toys, routine maintenance, and batteries are not included.)

1. What is this advertisement trying to sell you?

   _____

2. What does the advertisement say to convince you to buy this toy?

   A. It will make life easier.
   B. It will save you money.
   C. Everyone should have one.

3. What does the advertisement tell you is good about the toy?

   _____

   _____

   _____

   _____

4. Does the advertisement tell you anything bad about the toy?

   yes   **no**

5. What should you be careful about when buying this toy?

   _____

   _____

   _____

The Wright Brothers

Read the passage. Then, answer the questions.

Orville and Wilbur Wright are famous American brothers. They owned a bicycle shop in Dayton, Ohio. They also thought of flying. In 1899, they **experimented**, or tried new ideas, with flight. They started by testing kites. Then, they tested airplanes without motors. These airplanes were called gliders. These tests taught them how an airplane should move and fly. The brothers made more than 1,000 flights at a field in Kitty Hawk, North Carolina. The Wright brothers put a small engine on an airplane they named *Flyer*. On December 17, 1903, Orville Wright took the first flight using an airplane with a motor. The flight lasted 12 seconds. The brothers kept experimenting. Finally, they were able to stay in the air more than one hour.

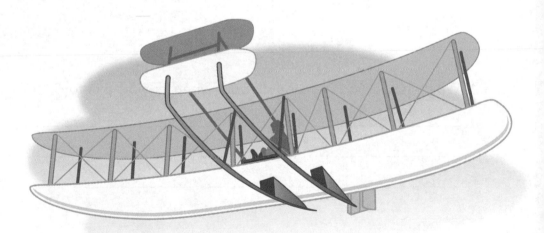

1. What is the main idea of the story?

    A. Testing new ideas is not important.
    B. The *Flyer* was the first airplane.
    C. The Wright brothers were early pilots.

2. What does the word **experiment** mean?

    A. to try new ideas
    B. to test kites
    C. to stay in the air for one hour

3. Where did the brothers test their gliders and their airplane?

    _____

4. How long did their first flight in an airplane with a motor last?

    _____

5. How did the brothers learn about what makes airplanes work?

    _____

    _____

    _____

Photograph

Read the story. Then, answer the questions.

Lamar was not comfortable. His new shirt was too stiff, and his tie felt tight. His mother had fussed over his hair. She wanted to make it look just right. She made him scrub his hands three times to clean the dirt from under his fingernails. Then, he had to brush and floss his teeth. Finally, his mom said he was ready. She smiled and said that Lamar looked very handsome. Lamar frowned, but he knew he could not tell his mom how he really felt. This was important to her. So, Lamar sat on a stool and looked toward the camera. He tried his best, even though he did not feel like smiling. "Perfect!" said the man behind the camera as he snapped the shot. The camera made a clicking sound. Lamar posed two more times. Then, the man said they were finished. The first thing Lamar did was take off his tie!

1. What was Lamar doing?

   _____

2. What clues tell you what Lamar is doing?

   _____

   _____

   _____

   _____

3. How does Lamar feel?

   A. excited

   B. uncomfortable

   C. sad

4. What clues tell you how Lamar feels?

   _____

   _____

   _____

   _____

5. The _____ said, "Perfect!"

Amelia Earhart

Read the passage. Then, complete the crossword puzzle.

It is not surprising that Amelia Earhart wanted to fly an airplane. She was fearless when she was a little girl. In 1920, not many women flew airplanes. She did not let that stop her.

She started flying lessons in 1921. In 1922, she set a record for the highest flight by a woman. Then, in 1928, a man asked her if she could cross the Atlantic Ocean in an airplane. Earhart said that she could. Charles Lindbergh was the first man to fly across the ocean in an airplane. Earhart became the first woman to fly across the Atlantic Ocean as a passenger. After the flight, people called her "Lady Lindy."

In 1932, she flew across the Atlantic Ocean again. This time she flew alone. In 1935, she was the first person to fly alone from Hawaii to California. She kept setting records. But, in 1937, she made the biggest news of all. Earhart was going to fly around the world!

Earhart and her navigator took off on June 1, 1937. They left from Florida. Her friends never dreamed it would be the last time they ever saw Earhart. On July 2, a ship picked up a radio call from Earhart somewhere over the Pacific Ocean. She said that she was running out of gas. They could not see the island where they were supposed to land for fuel. No one ever heard from them again.

We may never find the truth about the death of Amelia Earhart. But, she proved that women could have the same jobs as men and do them just as well.

1. Earhart disappeared over the _____ Ocean on July 2, 1937.

2. In 1928, Earhart became the first _____ to fly across the Atlantic Ocean as a passenger.

3. Earhart and her _____ took off on June 1, 1937.

4. Earhart started _____ in 1921.

5. Charles _____ was the first man to fly across the Atlantic Ocean.

6. People called Earhart "_____."

7. Earhart was the first _____ to fly alone from Hawaii to California.

8. In 1932, Earhart crossed the Atlantic Ocean _____ .

Notes

Read the notes. Then, answer the questions.

Shauna,
Your music teacher called to say that you left your math book in her room. She will leave it on the assistant's desk. Try to pick it up by 4:30.

Mom,
The carpet cleaning company called. They said that they are running late. They were supposed to come at 2:00. They are about one hour behind schedule.

Sam,
Your friend Jonathan called. He may not make it to the game because his sister broke her arm, and they are still at the hospital. He said you should ask William to play goalie if he does not make it back for the game.

Dad,
Uncle Harry called to say that he could not meet you at Pizza Joe's. Instead, he will meet you at the golf course after lunch.

1. What book did Shauna leave behind at her music lesson?

   A. music
   B. reading
   C. math

2. Where will Uncle Harry meet Dad?

   _____

3. The carpet cleaners should be there by what time?

   _____

4. What position does Jonathan play?

   _____

5. _____ broke her arm.

6. Whom should Sam ask to play goalie?

   A. Jonathan
   B. William
   C. Joe

7. Will the carpet cleaners be early or late?

   _____

Bats

Read the passage. Then, answer the questions.

Many people do not know all of the things that bats do for us. Bats are special animals. They are the only flying mammals on Earth. There are more than 900 kinds of bats in the world today. The smallest bat is also the smallest mammal. It is about the size of a bumblebee. The largest bat has a wingspan of up to 6 feet (1.83 m).

Bats help control the insect population. They use a sonar system to find and eat thousands of mosquitoes, mayflies, and moths at night. A bat makes a high-pitched sound that humans cannot hear. The sound bounces back and tells the bat where its next meal is.

Although most bats just eat insects, some eat fruit and the nectar of flowers. This is another way that bats are helpful. Bats pollinate flowers and spread the seeds for many tropical trees. Mango, cashew, and banana trees all depend on bats.

1. What is the main idea of this passage?

   _____

   _____

   _____

2. How many different kinds of bats are there in the world?
   A. more than 900
   B. more than 90
   C. more than 9,000

3. What do bats like to eat?

   _____

   _____

4. The largest species of bat has a wingspan of

   _____.

5. What kinds of tropical trees depend on bats to spread their seeds for pollination?

   _____

   _____

   _____

The Vanishing School Supplies

Read the story. Then, answer the questions in complete sentences.

"Mom, I need more pencils for school tomorrow. I think I should get a lot," Reba said as she jumped into the car.

"Wow, you must really be working hard," replied Reba's mother. "You have used so many school supplies already. Last week, you needed scissors, and the week before that, it was glue."

The next morning, Reba put two packages of brand-new pencils in her backpack. When her mother picked her up after school, Reba said, "Hey Mom, can we swing by the store to get more markers?"

"What?" Reba's mother asked. "Reba, what is going on? You cannot possibly be using all of your supplies this quickly."

"Well, I am sharing them. It all started when Ivy made fun of Shelby's binder. The cover was bent and dirty. It looked pretty bad. Then, Shelby said that her family could not buy her a new one until her mom got paid again. I started thinking about it and realized that Shelby never had her own scissors or glue. So, I gave her mine."

"Reba, I am very proud of you. I have an idea. We should invite Shelby to get ice cream with us after school tomorrow. I think you both deserve a little extra treat."

1. Why did Reba ask for so many new supplies?

   _____

   _____

2. What supplies did Reba share with Shelby?

   _____

   _____

   _____

3. Why did Shelby not have her own school supplies?

   _____

   _____

4. Why did Ivy make fun of Shelby's binder?

   A. She lost it.
   B. It had a silly picture on it.
   C. The cover was bent and dirty.

5. Why did Reba's mom feel proud of her daughter?

   _____

   _____

   _____

Ducks with Motors

Read the passage. Then, answer the questions in complete sentences.

Ducks can go from land to water. This is true for the bird. It is also true for the trucks and cars called *ducks*. You may have seen a duck in a spy movie. But, this water-to-land transportation is real.

The American, German, and British militaries used ducks during World War II. The first ducks were big, heavy trucks shaped like tanks. The huge trucks could take troops and supplies from a ship to the land. The trucks could drive onto land from the water. They were big and slow, but they helped keep soldiers safe.

After the war, some people in the United States bought ducks. They were used for tourist rides. In cities like Philadelphia, Pennsylvania, you can ride in a duck. The duck takes you to sights on land. Then, it drives into the water!

1. Where can a duck vehicle drive?

   A. land and water
   B. land
   C. water

2. According to the passage, when were ducks used by the military?

   _____

   _____

3. Why were the ducks important to the military?

   _____

   _____

   _____

4. Today, ducks are used in cities like _____ .

5. How are ducks used today?

   _____

   _____

Janek's Party

Read the paragraph and the invitation. Then, answer the questions.

Janek is a third grader in Ms. Valdez's class. When Janek was five years old, his family moved from Warsaw, Poland, to Austin, Texas. Janek likes the warm weather, and he loves to swim. He is having a pool party at the end of the school year. He and his mom made invitations for the party. Janek is sending this invitation to everyone in his class:

A Pool Party

Your friend Janek is having a party.
Please join us!

When: Saturday, May 29
What time: 12:00 noon until 3:00 p.m.
Where: Splash Time Kids' Pool and Picnic Grounds

Please bring a swimsuit, a towel, and sunscreen. We will play in the pool and then have a picnic. (If it rains, we will have an indoor party at Janek's house.)
Parents are welcome! Please respond by calling 555-7878. See you Saturday!

Directions:
1. Take Highway 1, heading south.
2. Exit at Lake Austin Boulevard.
3. Make a right at the first traffic light.
4. Drive two blocks and make a left onto Splash Time Drive.
5. Drive down the hill and park in the parking lot.

1. This selection is mostly about

   A. where to take swimming lessons.
   B. Ms. Valdez's third-grade class.
   C. how Janek invites kids to a party.

2. Which of the following items should people bring to Janek's party?

   A. sandwiches
   B. towels
   C. balloons

3. If it rains, the party will

   A. be canceled.
   B. be moved to a place indoors.
   C. take place another day.

4. According to the directions, what should you do after exiting at Lake Austin Boulevard?

   A. Take Highway 1, heading north.
   B. Make a right at the first traffic light.
   C. Make a left at the first traffic light.

5. The invitation asks people to

   A. call to say if they are coming.
   B. bring blankets for a picnic.
   C. prepare songs to sing for Janek.

Marc Brown

Read the passage. Then, answer the questions.

Marc Brown is the best-selling author of the Arthur books. You may have read *Arthur's Birthday*, *D. W. Thinks Big*, or *Arthur and the True Francine*. These books and others tell about the life of an aardvark, his family, and his quirky animal friends.

Brown enjoys drawing and telling stories. His grandmother, Grandma Thora, told wonderful stories too. Brown got his love of storytelling from her. He especially liked to tell animal stories to his own sons, who are now adults. One day, he told a story about an aardvark named Arthur. That was how the Arthur stories started.

From the time he was six years old, Brown enjoyed drawing. Grandma Thora loved his drawings. She saved his drawings and told him to draw more. Now, Brown draws the pictures and writes all of the stories for the Arthur books.

The first Arthur book was published in 1976. That book was called *Arthur's Nose*. In that book, Arthur had a long nose like a real aardvark. In the more recent books, Arthur's nose has gotten smaller. Brown shrank Arthur's nose so that he could show more expressions on Arthur's face. Since that first book, Brown has written more than 75 books!

The ideas for the Arthur stories come from Brown's experiences as a child. He also gets ideas from his three children, Tolon, Tucker, and Eliza. In many of Brown's books, you can find the names of his sons, Tolon and Tucker. The next time you read an Arthur book, see if you can find their names!

1. What does Marc Brown love to do?

   _____

2. Where does Brown get some of the ideas for the Arthur stories?

   A. from the zoo
   B. from going on vacation
   C. from his children

3. Where did Brown get his love of storytelling?

   _____

4. If you could ask Brown one question, what would you ask?

   _____

   _____

5. Imagine you are a writer and an artist like Marc Brown. Draw your own storybook character in the space below. Then, on a separate sheet of paper, write a story about your character.

Wolfgang Amadeus Mozart

Read the passage. Then, number the events in the order in which they happened.

Some people seem to be born with talent. That was true of the composer Wolfgang Amadeus Mozart. When he was three years old, Mozart started to play songs on the piano. When he was five, he started to write his own music. His father was a musician too. He took the young Mozart to the royal courts of kings and queens. Mozart played all over Europe. He could play perfectly, even while wearing a blindfold!

Mozart started to publish his music when he was only seven years old. By the time he was eight, he had taught himself how to play the organ and the violin. He also wrote a symphony, a full-length piece of music, when he was eight. He was only 13 years old when he wrote his first opera. An opera is acted out like a play with singing parts instead of speaking parts.

When he was an adult, he was one of the most famous composers of all time. His works are still played and loved all over the world today.

1. _____ Mozart started playing the piano.

2. _____ Mozart taught himself to play the organ and the violin.

3. _____ Mozart wrote his first opera.

4. _____ Mozart started publishing his music.

5. _____ Mozart started writing his own music.

6. _____ Mozart wrote his first symphony.

Horace Mann

Read the passage. Then, write *F* if a statement is a fact. Write *O* if a statement is an opinion.

Horace Mann was a Massachusetts state senator. In 1835, he voted to create the first state board of education in the United States. He was surprised and honored when he was chosen to lead the board in 1837. He took his new job very seriously. No one had ever done this job before. He went around the state visiting many schools. He even went to Europe to learn how their schools were run. He wanted to know how to make the schools in his state better.

Horace Mann led the Massachusetts Board of Education to build a system of schools for all children. These schools were different in many ways. Their school year lasted six months, not just two or three. Teachers started attending special colleges to learn how to teach. He also started district libraries so that students would have many books to read. Other states saw the nice, new schools in Massachusetts. They wanted good schools for their children too. Soon, many states created school boards of education.

1. _____ A good school system is the most important part of a democracy.

2. _____ Horace Mann was a Massachusetts state senator.

3. _____ Mann voted to create the first state board of education in the United States.

4. _____ Europe still has better schools than the United States.

5. _____ Mann headed the first state board of education in the United States.

6. _____ Under Mann's leadership, the length of the school year doubled.

7. _____ Mann went to Europe to see their schools and to talk with experts about education.

My Shadow
by Robert Louis Stevenson

Read the poem. Then, answer the questions.

1   I HAVE a little shadow that goes in and out with me,
    And what can be the use of him is more than I can see.
    He is very, very like me from the heels up to the head;
    And I see him jump before me, when I jump into my bed.

5   The funniest thing about him is the way he likes to grow–
    Not at all like proper children, which is always very slow;
    For he sometimes shoots up taller like an India-rubber ball,
    And he sometimes gets so little that there's none of him at all.

    He hasn't got a notion of how children ought to play,
10   And can only make a fool of me in every sort of way.
    He stays so close beside me, he's a coward you can see;
    I'd think shame to stick to nursie as that shadow sticks to me!

    One morning, very early, before the sun was up,
    I rose and found the shining dew on every buttercup;
15   But my lazy little shadow, like an arrant* sleepy-head,
    Had stayed at home behind me and was fast asleep in bed.

* that is, extreme (a real sleepy-head)

1. Which sentence best tells what the poem is about?

   A. A child goes to school and discovers his shadow.
   B. A child thinks about bird and animal shadows.
   C. A child describes his relationship with his shadow.

2. Which word best describes how the speaker feels about his shadow?

   A. quiet   B. amused   C. bored

3. The shadow is different from the speaker because it can

   A. get bigger and smaller.
   B. jump up and down.
   C. play outside and inside.

4. What happens in the last stanza of the poem (lines 13–16)?

   A. The speaker goes to sleep.
   B. The speaker meets a new friend.
   C. The shadow stays at home.

5. Why did Stevenson write this poem?

   A. to explain how to make shadow animals on a wall
   B. to entertain readers with a familiar topic
   C. to inform readers about the types of shadows

The Human Body

Read the table of contents. Then, write the chapter number and the page number where you would begin looking for the answer to each question.

Table of Contents

		Chapter	Page
1.	How long does it take a bite of pizza to reach your stomach?		
2.	How does your body know when something tastes sour?		
3.	How many bones are in your skeleton?		
4.	What color is your blood?		
5.	How can you make yourself stronger?		
6.	How fast do nerve impulses travel?		
7.	Why do you have a belly button?		
8.	Are there more bones in your hand or your foot?		
9.	About how far can humans see?		
10.	How much of your body is made of water?		

Campfire Walking Salad

Read the recipe. Then, draw the steps for making a walking salad. Explain the steps and label the ingredients in your drawing.

Before you pick up your hot dog at the campfire, make a walking salad. You will not need a fork or plate for this salad. Just wrap the ingredients in a piece of lettuce and you are ready to go!

Ingredients:

- large lettuce leaves
- salted peanuts
- marshmallows
- peanut butter
- raisins
- coconut shavings

Directions: Wash and pat dry several leaves of lettuce. Choose a lettuce leaf and spread peanut butter on it. Then, add spoonfuls of the other toppings. Roll up the lettuce leaf like a tortilla. Eat and enjoy!

1

2

3

4

Helen Keller

Read the passage. Then, answer the questions.

Helen Keller was a famous woman. She was born in 1880. When she was 19 months old, she had a serious illness that left her unable to speak, hear, or see. For many years after that, young Keller lived in complete darkness and silence. She acted wildly. No one could get through to her.

Then, Keller met her new teacher, Ann Sullivan. Keller was just seven years old. Sullivan taught her to "hear" and "speak" with her hands. Keller learned quickly. She even learned to use her voice. Keller went on to college and graduated with honors in 1904.

Keller was very smart and hardworking. She wrote books and gave speeches. Keller did not let her disabilities stop her from doing anything she wanted to do. She also taught others how to live with disabilities. She worked to make life fair and safe for people who have different abilities. Helen Keller lived to be 88 years old.

1. An accomplishment is a goal that someone completes. List four of Helen Keller's greatest accomplishments.

   _____

   _____

   _____

   _____

2. Choose one of Keller's accomplishments. Explain why you think it was harder for her to do than it would be for a hearing, sighted person.

   _____

   _____

   _____

3. Write four words that describe Helen Keller.

   _____   _____

   _____   _____

4. Imagine you could not see, hear, or talk. What would be different about your day? Explain one change that you would have to make in the morning, the afternoon, and the evening.

   Morning: _____

   Afternoon: _____

   Evening: _____

Colorful Bait

Read the passage. Then, answer the questions.

A clown fish has **vibrant** stripes and colors just like a clown. That is probably where it got the name. There are many different patterns and colors on the bodies of clown fish. The most common is orange with white and black stripes.

Real clown fish are not funny. They are **fierce**. They protect their homes and their eggs with care. A female clown fish lays between 300 and 700 eggs at one time. But, a male clown fish takes care of the eggs. He watches them until they hatch.

Clown fish have strange homes. They live in the **tentacles** of a sea animal called an anemone. These two animals have made a deal with each other. The anemone provides a safe home and does not eat the clown fish. In return, a clown fish does three things for the anemone. The clown fish cleans the anemone's tentacles by eating leftover bits of food. It guards the anemone against some enemies. And, the clown fish acts as bait. The clown fish's bright stripes **tempt** other fish to come toward the poisonous tentacles. Then, the anemone stings these fish and eats them. The **alliance** between these two sea animals works very well for both of them.

1. What does the word **vibrant** mean as it is used in the passage?

    A. white   B. colorless C. bright

2. What does the word **fierce** mean as it is used in the passage?

    A. powerful   B. lazy   C. weak

3. What does the word **tentacles** mean as it is used in the passage?

    A. arms   B. eyes   C. stomachs

4. What does the word **tempt** mean as it is used in the passage?

    A. frighten   B. attract   C. bore

5. What does the word **alliance** mean as it is used in the passage?

    A. conversation B. fight   C. agreement

Colorado Attractions

Read the passage. Then, write the topic sentence from each paragraph and two details that support the topic sentence.

Pike's Peak is located in the Rocky Mountains of Colorado. The Rocky Mountains are a mountain range in the western part of the United States. Pike's Peak is not the highest mountain peak in the state. But, it is well known for the view from the top of the mountain. You can visit the peak and climb the mountain. People get to the top by walking, riding the cog railway, or driving a car.

Pike's Peak was named after the first American explorer to see it. His name was Zebulon Pike. He explored the southwestern area of the United States. He first saw the mountain in 1806.

The Royal Gorge is a deep canyon. The canyon was created by the rain and snow that run off the mountains and into the rivers. The Arkansas River runs through the bottom of the canyon. The bottom of Royal Gorge is more than 1,000 feet (305 m) deep! There is a bridge that crosses the canyon. Visitors like to walk out on the bridge to enjoy the view.

Paragraph 1

Topic Sentence:

_____

_____

Supporting Detail:

_____

_____

Supporting Detail:

_____

_____

Paragraph 2

Topic Sentence:

_____

_____

Supporting Detail:

_____

_____

Supporting Detail:

_____

_____

Now or Then?

Read the passage. Then, answer the questions.

Have you ever been in a convertible car? If you had lived long ago when Henry Ford started making cars, you probably would have been in a convertible car. Ford built the first cars that many people could afford to buy. He made cars in a new way that cost less money. That made the cars cheaper for people to buy. The cars could not go as fast as the cars we drive today. But, they did help people get where they needed to go.

Ford's cars were a little different from today's cars. The gas tank was under the driver's seat. A person had to lift the seat out to put gas in the car! Sometimes, a car would not start in cold weather. So, people had to pour hot water under the hood. Many of the cars did not have bumpers or mirrors. That was because they cost extra money. Ford's cars were a way to move people around, just like our cars today.

Would you rather have a car from the past or a car from today? Make a list of similarities and differences to help you decide.

1. How cars of the past and cars of today are alike:

   _____

   _____

   _____

   _____

2. How cars of the past and cars of today are different:

   _____

   _____

   _____

   _____

3. Based on your lists, would you rather have a car from the past or a car from today?

   _____

   _____

James Cook

Read the passage. Then, answer the questions.

In 1768, James Cook sailed a long way for a strange reason. Scientists found a way to see how far the sun was from the earth. To help them test this idea, Cook would sail from England to an island in the South Pacific Ocean. He and his crew would then measure the time it took the planet Venus to move across the sun.

There were 94 people on Cook's ship. Eleven of the people on the ship were scientists. The ship's name was the *Endeavor*. Their trip was very long. Cook did everything he could to keep his crew healthy. He made the crew keep their beds clean. He brought fruits and vegetables for them to eat. Cook even kept a goat onboard to give them milk!

They reached the island of Tahiti after eight months at sea. They found friendly people there. The crew watched Venus as they were told. Then, it was time to go. Cook had a new mission for them. They wanted to see if they could find a new **continent**. For many years, mapmakers believed that there was another continent the size of Asia. Cook did not find what he was looking for. Instead, he landed on New Zealand and the eastern coast of Australia.

When Cook returned home, he was famous for his discoveries. James Cook was a new kind of explorer. He did not want to harm the people he met during his travels or take away their land. Instead, he looked for new things to learn about.

1. Choose a good title for this passage.

    A. The Path of Venus
    B. Exploring for Science
    C. The Lost Continent

2. How long did it take the *Endeavor* to reach Tahiti?

    _____

3. What was Cook unable to find after they left Tahiti?

    _____

4. What did Cook have on the ship to keep the crew healthy?

    _____

5. What was the *Endeavor's* crew supposed to do in Tahiti?

    _____

6. Number the events in the order in which they happened.

    _____ Cook became famous for the things he discovered.

    _____ The *Endeavor* started searching for a new continent.

    _____ Cook left England for the South Pacific.

    _____ The *Endeavor* reached Tahiti.

    _____ The *Endeavor* reached Australia.

7. What does the word **continent** mean?

    A. a major landmass
    B. an ocean
    C. a mountain

Tissue-Eating Disease

Read the passage. Then, answer the questions.

Vance "Bo" Salisbury was sick because of a rare tissue-eating disease. Only a few people get this disease each year. Germs getting into a cut or sore cause this disease. If a person gets a cut or sore and treats it properly and quickly, he will not get sick.

One day, Salisbury hurt his ankle. The next day, the pain was so bad that his wife took him to the hospital. The doctors did not know what was wrong with him. So, they sent him home. The next day, his stomach was upset and he could not walk. He went back to the hospital, and his doctor started doing tests.

Salisbury kept getting worse. Finally, the doctors knew what was wrong. Salisbury had gotten a tissue-eating disease. They would have to give him strong medicine quickly to stop the disease. Everyone was worried. Suddenly, the disease stopped spreading. The doctors said that it was a miracle.

To make sure all of the germs were gone, the doctors operated on Salisbury's leg. They also replaced some of the tissue that the disease had ruined.

Today, Salisbury's leg is healthy. He runs two or three miles each day. He is back at work and glad to be a survivor.

1. Choose another title for the story.

   A. Going Home
   B. Leg Injuries
   C. An Unusual Disease

2. Why did the doctors replace some of Salisbury's leg tissue?

   _____

   _____

3. How do you know that Salisbury's leg is healthy today?

   _____

   _____

4. Number the events in the order in which they happened.

   _____ Salisbury went back to work.

   _____ Salisbury went to the hospital but was sent home.

   _____ Salisbury hurt his ankle.

   _____ Some of the tissue on Salisbury's leg was replaced.

   _____ The doctors started running tests.

5. What can you tell about tissue-eating disease after reading about Salisbury and his experience with the disease?

   A. You can only get the disease in your leg.
   B. It is difficult for doctors to diagnose the disease, but once they do, it can be treated.
   C. If you think you have it, it is best to wait before going to the hospital.

A Camping Trip

Read the story. Then, answer the questions.

Tyrone and his family went on a camping trip. They found the perfect spot beside a creek. Tyrone and his sister set up the tent. Their mom and dad got out the supplies for dinner. When camp was set up, Tyrone told his parents that he wanted to go exploring in the creek while the sun was still up. His father told him not to go too far from their campsite and to be careful.

Tyrone rolled up his pant legs and waded into the water. He used a stick to poke a few leaves and rocks on the creek bed. Pretty soon, he saw something that looked back at him. It was a snake! Tyrone leaped out of the water and raced down the dirt path back to camp. Tyrone jumped into the car and closed the door.

1. How did Tyrone feel when he saw the snake? How do you know?

   _____

   _____

   _____

   _____

2. Number the events in the order in which they happened.

   _____ Tyrone waded into the water.

   _____ Tyrone helped his sister set up the tent.

   _____ Tyrone jumped into the car and closed the door.

   _____ Tyrone saw a snake in the creek.

   _____ Tyrone told his parents he wanted to explore in the creek.

3. What do you think Tyrone did next? Finish the story.

   _____

   _____

   _____

   _____

   _____

   _____

   _____

   _____

Ruby Bridges

Read the passage. Then, answer the questions.

Have you ever not wanted to go to school? What if you knew that when you got to school, adults would yell at you to leave? What if you were only six years old when this happened?

That is exactly what happened to Ruby Bridges on Monday, November 14, 1960. That was the day the public schools in New Orleans were **integrated**. Bridges was the first African American child to go to an elementary school that was once only for white people.

Bridges's parents wanted her to go to a good school. The best school was just five blocks away from their home. However, it was only for white students. It took a new law, an order from a judge, and many police officers to see that Bridges could start going to that school.

The people in the city were not happy. They tried to get Bridges to stay home. People made threats to hurt her family. Bridges's father was fired from his job.

On that first day, Bridges waited in an office all day. On her second day, she went to her classroom. She met her teacher, Mrs. Henry. The white parents had kept their children home. Bridges was Mrs. Henry's only student all year.

Bridges worked hard and got good grades. She grew up and went into business. She even helps at her old school. What she did helped all children today have a chance for a better education.

1. Choose another title for this story.

    A. Equal Education for All
    B. Study Hard and You Will Do Well
    C. Good Schools Are Hard to Find

2. How far away did Ruby Bridges live from the school her parents wanted her to attend?

    _____

3. In what city did Bridges live?

    _____

4. What happened to Bridges's father when she started at the new school?

    _____

5. Number the events in the order in which they happened.

    _____ A law was passed integrating public schools.

    _____ Bridges entered an all-white school.

    _____ Bridges waited in the principal's office on her first day of school.

    _____ Bridges went to business school.

    _____ Bridges met Mrs. Henry.

6. What does the word **integrated** mean?

    A. mixed
    B. decided
    C. separated

Francisco Vásquez de Coronado

Read the passage. Then, answer the questions.

Francisco Vásquez de Coronado was an explorer for Spain. He was also the governor of New Spain. New Spain was the old name for Mexico. Coronado heard of the seven cities of gold. They were called the Seven Cities of Cibola. He heard they were full of gold and jewels, but no one knew where to find these cities. Coronado wanted to find these cities. He wanted to take all of their gold for Spain.

In 1540, Spain owned a large part of Mexico. The land north of Mexico was unknown. Only a few explorers had **ventured** into that land. Coronado thought the seven cities of gold might be there. So, he decided to start looking in that area.

Coronado led a group of 1,300 people. They looked for gold in the area that is now the state of Arizona. There they met a tribe of American Indians. They were the Zuni tribe. Coronado thought their city might have the gold. But, the Zuni tribe was poor. No gold was there.

Coronado still wanted to find gold. He sent his people in groups to look for the cities of gold. One group found the Grand Canyon. Another group found more American Indian villages. Coronado's people found many new things. But, they did not find gold.

In 1542, Coronado led his people home. He had looked for two years, and he was tired and sad. He was not famous for all of his hard work. He was called a failure. He even lost his job as governor.

Today, people remember Coronado as an explorer. He was the first European to explore the North American southwest.

1. Which of the following best describes Coronado?

   A. friendly   B. greedy   C. angry

2. What was the name for the seven cities of gold?

   _____

3. What was Mexico called when Coronado was the governor?

   _____

4. Number the events in the order in which they happened.

   _____ Coronado heard about the seven cities of gold.

   _____ Coronado met the Zuni tribe.

   _____ Coronado entered what is now the state of Arizona.

   _____ Coronado was called a failure.

   _____ A group of Coronado's men discovered the Grand
   Canyon.

5. What does the word **ventured** mean?

   A. dared to go   B. escaped   C. settled

6. Why do you think Coronado was called a failure when he
   returned home?

   A. He did not discover the Grand Canyon himself.
   B. He did not find any gold on his journey.
   C. He did not conquer the seven cities of gold.

What Does It Mean?

Read each paragraph. Then, circle the best meaning for the bold word or phrase.

1. Sierra was having a party. She wanted to know how many people would come, so she wrote **RSVP** and her phone number on each invitation.

    A. Bring a present.
    B. Please reply.
    C. Please call if you are going to be late.

2. Every week, Drew's father gave him an allowance of $1.00. One week, Andrew got $5.00 from his father.

    "Will I get five dollars every week?" Drew asked.

    "No," his father said. "Just **once in a blue moon**."

    A. once a month
    B. when the moon is blue
    C. every once in a while

3. Zach put off getting ready for the class trip until the last minute. He had to hurry. David was waiting for him. After they got on the bus, Zach remembered that his shoes were still under his bed! The whole class had to wait for him. "**Haste makes waste**, Zach," his teacher said.

    A. Trash should always be recycled.
    B. Hurrying too much can cost you even more time later.
    C. Always hurry when you are throwing away trash.

4.   When Alexander moved, he made many new friends, but he did not forget his old pals. One weekend, he invited Carlos and Ryan, two friends from his old school, to come for a visit. He also invited Jawan and Noah, two of his new friends. At first, Carlos and Ryan were very quiet. Alexander was confused. He thought they would all have fun together. Then, Alexander had an idea. He grabbed his bat and baseball. They all went to the park. It really **broke the ice**. After they hit a few balls, all of the boys were talking and laughing as if they had known each other since first grade.

A.   made them nervous
B.   helped them relax
C.   improved their game

5.   Abigail was having the best day of her life. First, she got an A on her history report. Then, she got a lot of compliments about her new jeans. Finally, her best friend announced that her family was not moving to Ohio like they had planned. Abigail looked out the window and smiled. Her teacher patted her on the back. "**Everything is coming up roses**," she said. "I have had days like this too."

A.   When one thing goes right, many things seem to go right.
B.   Things go right, and then the roses bloom.
C.   It is always a good day when you get an A on a report.

A Mixed-Up Story

Read the sentences. Then, number the sentences to put the story in order.

_____ Carla and her friends sat together on the bus.

_____ Her mom dropped her off at the school.

_____ When Carla woke up, she was excited about the class picnic.

_____ She loaded her backpack into her mom's car and jumped in the back seat.

_____ The bus left the school on time. The trip had begun!

_____ Her friends Michelle and Anna were waiting for her at the school.

_____ She packed some sunscreen, a hat, and her lunch into her backpack.

Make a Word

How many new words can you make using the letters in the words below? The first one is started for you.

FLOWERPOT	NOTEBOOK
top	
owe	

FRIENDSHIP

Make it a contest! Have a friend write the same three words on a separate sheet of paper. See who can come up with the most new words. Or, set a time limit to see who can think of more words in a certain amount of time.

Homophone Word Search

Read the following words. Write the homophone for each word on the line. Then, find and circle your answers in the word search. Words may be found across, down, or diagonally.

Homophones are words that sound the same but have different meanings.

1. dear _____

2. hare_____

3. pail _____

4. sea_____

5. tow _____

6. flee _____

7. blew _____

8. feat _____

9. tale _____

10. plain _____

a	r	h	l	d	e	e	r
p	d	i	m	e	x	l	y
b	a	k	u	m	n	t	f
t	k	l	h	e	g	s	l
r	b	c	e	b	w	d	e
h	t	z	o	l	j	f	a
a	s	p	l	a	n	e	h
i	l	h	y	v	s	e	e
r	e	t	o	e	a	t	k

Using Context Clues

Each pair of sentences contains a nonsense word. Write a word on the line that makes sense in place of the nonsense word.

1. Green is my favorite **prackle**.
   My cousin likes to **prackle** with markers and crayons.

   The nonsense word **prackle** means _____.

2. Nadia likes to **verg** her bicycle after school.
   I think the best **verg** at the amusement park is the carousel.

   The nonsense word **verg** means _____.

3. Hector likes to **jeffa** soccer at the park on the weekend.
   My sister, Alicia, was the lead in the school **jeffa** this year.

   The nonsense word **jeffa** means _____.

4. My friend and I **blape** a good movie last weekend.
   Jasper's dad used a small **blape** to cut down the tree by their house.

   The nonsense world **blape** means _____.

Answer Key

Page 5
1. F; 2. F; 3. T; 4. T; 5. F; 6. F; 7. T

Page 7
1. a skunk; 2. effect, cause; 3. She wants to win the Costume Day contest.; 4. Answers will vary.

Page 9
1. A.; 2. His bicycle does not have training wheels, and he cannot read yet.; 3. yard sale; 4. It was messy. Alexa is surprised he can ever find anything.; 5. five-dollar bill; 6. No, she has to use the coin laundry.

Page 10
3, 6, 1, 5, 4, 2

Page 11
1. B.; 2. B.; 3. C.; 4. B.; 5. A.

Page 12
1. a palm tree; 2. no; 3. the ocean; 4. redwood; 5. at least 2,000 years

Page 13
1. A.; 2. C.

Pages 14–15
1. Big Mystery Solved!; 2. Dinosaur Wins Dream House!; 3. Local Author Writes Book!; 4. Time Runs Out for Della's Drive; 5. Prowler Caught by Police

Page 17
1. B.; 2. C.; 3. B.; 4. B.

Page 18
1. B.; 2. C.; 3. A.; 4. C.; 5. B.

Page 19
1. A.; 2. A.; 3. B.; 4. C.; 5. A.

Page 21
1. F; 2. F; 3. O; 4. F; 5. F; Details can include: were here before dinosaurs; have good hearing; have good eyesight; can go days without water; eat almost anything; can go weeks without food; give birth to more than 100 babies in their short lifetimes (about one year)

Page 23
Details may include: There were no female astronauts when Ochoa was young.; Six women joined when Ochoa was in college.; Ochoa joined the space program in 1990.; Ochoa was the first Hispanic American woman in space.; She has been on three more missions since then.

Page 25
1. a Huggable Pet toy; 2. C.; 3. It can do tricks, you do not have to feed or bathe it, it snuggles with you, it comes when you call it, and it comes in a variety of animals.; 4. no; 5. extra costs, some assembly required

Page 27
1. C.; 2. A.; 3. Kitty Hawk, North Carolina; 4. about 12 seconds; 5. by experimenting with kites and gliders and then airplanes with motors

Page 29
1. He was having his picture taken.; 2. Clues may include: sitting on the stool, looking at the camera, posing two more times; 3. B.; 4. His shirt was too stiff, his tie was too tight, and he frowned.; 5. photographer

Answer Key

Page 31

(Crossword)
3. NAVIGATOR
4. FLYING LESSONS
6. LADY LINDY
7. PERSON
8. AGAIN

Down: 1. PACIFIC; 2. WOMAN; 5. LINBERGH; 6. L

Page 33

1. C.; 2. at the golf course; 3. by 3:00; 4. goalie; 5. Jonathan's sister; 6. B.; 7. late

Page 35

1. Bats do many things for people.; 2. A.; 3. Bats eat insects, fruit, and the nectar of flowers.; 4. up to 6 feet (1.83 m); 5. Bats spread seeds for mango, cashew, and banana trees.

Page 37

1. She was giving them to Shelby.; 2. pencils, scissors, glue, markers; 3. Her family could not afford to buy supplies.; 4. C.; 5. Reba had helped Shelby by sharing supplies with her.

Page 39

1. A.; 2. during World War II; 3. take troops and supplies to land, protect soldiers; 4. Philadelphia; 5. tourist rides

Page 41

1. C.; 2. B.; 3. B.; 4. B.; 5. A.

Page 43

1. He loves to draw and write.; 2. C.; 3. from his Grandma Thora; 4–5. Answers will vary.

Page 45

1, 4, 6, 3, 2, 5

Page 47

1. O; 2. F; 3. F; 4. O; 5. F; 6. F; 7. F

Page 49

1. C.; 2. B.; 3. A.; 4. C.; 5. B.

Page 51

1. 4, 51; 2. 7, 90; 3. 1, 3; 4. 5, 64; 5. 2, 25; 6. 3, 39; 7. 6, 72; 8. 1, 3; 9. 7, 90; 10. 5, 64

Page 53

Pictures will vary but should show the steps in this order: 1. Wash and dry the lettuce.; 2. Spread peanut butter on the lettuce.; 3. Add other toppings.; 4. Roll up the lettuce like a tortilla and eat it.

Page 55

1. Answers will vary. Possible answers include: learned to speak with her hands, learned to speak with her voice, graduated from college with honors, wrote books, taught others, worked against unfairness.; 2. Answers will vary. Example: It was hard for Keller to learn to use her voice because she could not hear herself.; 3.–4. Answers will vary.

Page 57

1. C.; 2. A.; 3. A.; 4. B.; 5. C.

Page 59

TS—Pike's Peak is located in the Rocky Mountains of Colorado.; Supporting details will vary.
TS—The Royal Gorge is a deep canyon.; Supporting details will vary.

Answer Key

Page 61

Answers will vary. Possible answers include: 1. Alike: They both use gas. They are a great way to get around. They are both available as convertibles.; 2. Different: Old cars could not go very fast. In old cars, the gas tank was under the front seat. Some old cars did not have bumpers or mirrors.; 3. Answers will vary.

Page 63

1. B.; 2. eight months; 3. a continent the size of Asia; 4. fruits and vegetables, and milk from a goat; 5. measure the time for Venus to cross the sun; 6. 5, 3, 1, 2, 4; 7. A.

Page 65

1. C.; 2. the disease had ruined it; 3. he runs two or three miles each day; 4. 5, 2, 1, 4, 3; 5. B.

Page 67

1. Tyrone felt afraid. He leapt out of the water, ran down the path, and jumped into his family's car.; 2. 3, 1, 5, 4, 2; 3. Answers will vary.

Page 69

1. A.; 2. five blocks; 3. New Orleans; 4. He was fired from his job.; 5. 1, 2, 3, 5, 4; 6. A.

Page 71

1. B.; 2. Cibola; 3. New Spain; 4. 1, 3, 2, 5, 4; 5. A.; 6. B.

Pages 72–73

1. B.; 2. C.; 3. B.; 4. B.; 5. A.

Page 74

6, 4, 1, 3, 7, 5, 2

Page 75

Answers will vary but may include:
Flowerpot: flow, plow, prow, row, tow, low, ow, owl, few, pew, to, too, two, flower, lower, power, tower, towel, pot, plot, rot, lot, flop, top, lop, fool, pool, tool, foot, root, troop, loop; **Notebook:** note, not, ton, to, too, ten, book, took, nook, boot, bone, tone, bet, net; **Friendship:** friend(s), end(s), send, fend(s), rend(s), fried, shied, den(s), pen(s), hen(s), pie(s), die(s), ship, hip(s), dip(s), drip(s), rip(s), ripe, nip(s), din, dine(s), dish, fin(s), fine, fish, pin(s), pine(s), shred, shin, shine, hid, hide(s), rid, ride(s).

Page 76

1. deer; 2. hair; 3. pale; 4. see; 5. toe; 6. flea; 7. blue; 8. feet; 9. tail; 10. plane

Page 77

1. color; 2. ride; 3. play; 4. saw